DEER
HUNTING

for Kids

Andrew McMurdie

OUTDOOR
→ KIDS →

RED WOLF PRESS

For information about discounts, bulk purchases, or author visits, please send an email to reviewkidsbooks@gmail.com.

ISBN: 978-1-955731-02-7

Published by Red Wolf Press.

Edited by Dena McMurdie,
Designer: Andrew McMurdie and Dena McMurdie

First printing, May 2022.

DISCLAIMER

This book does not replace a hunter's safety certification course, and should not be used as such. The information provided is the opinion of the author. Hunters should obey all local laws and best practices.

PHOTO CREDITS

Key: BG - Background; LR - Left to right; TB - Top to bottom

DP - Depositphotos.com
IS - iStockphotos.com
DS - Dreamstime.com

Front cover TB: ©Avalon_Studio/IS, BG:somen/DP, ©MB-PROJEKT_Maciej_Bledowski/IS, ©KeithSzafranski/IS
Back cover TB: ©Kahj19/DP, BG:somen/DP
p1 BG: ©EEI_Tony/DP, p2-3 BG: ©EEI_Tony/DP, p4-5 BG: ©twildlife/IS, p4: ©karinanh/DP, p6-7 BG: ©EEI_Tony/DP, p7 TB: ©splendens/IS, ©Shaiith79/DP, ©twildlife/DP, p8-9 BG: ©DelmasLehman/DP, LR: ©KeithSzafranski/IS, ©PantherMediaSeller/DP, p10: ©David McGowen/IS, p11: ©Jeff Edwards/IS, p12-13 BG ©Fertnig/IS, p13 TB: ©YAY-Images/DP, ©PixelsAway/DP, ©mybaitshop/DP, p14-15 BG: ©milehightraveler/IS, p15 TB: ©Ruhuntn/DS, ©Michael Olson/IS, p16-17 BG: ©Mike-Mareen/IS, p16 TB: ©sk-howard/IS, ©EXTREME-PHO-TOGRAPHER/IS, p18-19 BG: ©Kerry Hargrove/IS, p19 TB: ©Jeffrey Banke/DS, ©Tim Bingham/DS, ©StephanieFrey/DP, p20-21 BG: ©ehrlif/IS, p20: ©romankosolapov/DP, p22-23 BG: ©ElviK/IS, p23 TB: ©jimkruger/IS, ©schlag/DP, ©twildlife/DP, p24-25 BG: ©KeithSzafranski/IS, p25 TB: ©twildlife/DP, ©schlag/DP, ©AdamLongSculpture/IS, p26 TB: ©Pilligrim/DP, ©Jeffrey Banke/DS, p27: ©Fertnig/IS, p28-29 BG: ©yacobchuk1/DP, p29: ©RichLegg/IS, p30-31 BG: ©twildlife/IS, LR: ©peterwey/DP, ©fogbird/DP, p32-33 BG: ©Fertnig/IS, p33 TB: ©Andrew McMurdie, ©Monkey Business Images/DS, p34 TB/LR: ©Dena McMurdie, ©enterlinedesign/DP, ©Kanati Studio, ©mikeledray/DP, p35: ©Premek/DP, p36-37 BG: ©twildlife/DP, p38 TB: ©EEI_Tony/DP, ©Andrew McMurdie

TABLE OF CONTENTS

ON THE HUNT

Deer hunting has been part of North American culture for hundreds of years, and you get to carry on that tradition. The memory of harvesting your first deer will last a lifetime and give you a story to pass on to other hunters. This book will cover hunting both the mule deer and the whitetail deer.

LOCATION, LOCATION, LOCATION!

Whitetail deer:
Found throughout the US, Southern Canada, and most of Mexico.

Mule deer:
Found west of the Missouri River, near the Rocky Mountains from Canada to Mexico.

HUNTING IS AWESOME!

Hunting is a challenge! A successful hunt involves strategy, skill, and a bit of luck. But even if you don't get the big one on your first try, you'll still bring home priceless memories.

Nature
Watching the sunrise, listening to birds wake up, and the smell of pine trees are things you can only experience in nature.

Lifelong friendships

Deer hunting with family and friends builds strong bonds. Sharing food around a camp-fire and telling stories from past hunts creates lifelong memories.

Mmm, yummy!

Venison (deer meat) has 50% less fat than beef, is packed with protein, and is delicious!

The challenge

Hunting deer is difficult and requires a lot of skill. You'll have to put in plenty of time and effort to succeed.

AN AMAZING ANIMAL

Deer are incredible animals, and hunting them requires you to know and respect them. Here are some cool facts about deer.

Jump around

Whitetail deer can jump up to 12 feet high—4 feet higher than the human World Record. Likewise, mule deer can leap up to 15 feet long—3 feet longer than the human World Record.

Super sniffer

Deer have a better sense of smell than a bloodhound and can smell you up to a half-mile away. You'll need to stay downwind from them to avoid their powerful noses.

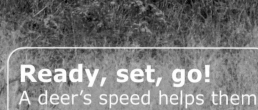

Ready, set, go!

A deer's speed helps them get away from predators. They can run in bursts of up to 35 miles per hour.

I.D. YOUR DEER

Identifying the different deer species is an essential skill for hunters.

Antler tines grow off of one main beam

Brown face with lighter rings around the eyes and nose

Brown bottom

Reddish-brown coat

The underside of the tail is white. They raise their tails to alert other deer to danger.

WHITETAIL DEER

Forked antlers

Antlers are often taller and wider than a whitetail's

Large ears

Light-colored face with a dark forehead

Grey-brown coat

White bottom with a black-tipped tail

MULE DEER

SCOUT LIKE A PRO

Finding deer isn't easy. However, because deer often stay in one area, you can scout them weeks or months in advance. You'll learn their patterns and improve your chances of success when hunting season arrives.

Pro tip!
Talking to other people is the easiest way to find a good hunting spot. Farmers, other hunters, and delivery workers often see deer and know where they are.

Follow the footprints

Keep your eyes open for deer tracks. They guarantee deer have been in the area and can show you travel patterns.

Oh crap!

Yes, even deer poop is useful. If you find a lot of droppings, that means it's a good hunting spot.

Smile, you're on camera!

A trail cam can give you proof that deer are in the area. It can also show you if any big bucks are roaming around.

BE A DEER DETECTIVE

Snow is a hunter's best friend. It makes deer easier to spot and track.

Scrapes

Bucks paw the ground, then urinate on it to leave their scent during the rut. Look for bare spots of earth where deer have scraped away the sticks and leaves.

Rubs

Bucks rub their antlers on trees to mark their territory and intimidate other males. Keep your eye out for trees with missing patches of bark. Fresh rubs and scrapes are good signs a buck is in the area.

STAY HIDDEN

Now that you know how to find deer, you need to choose the best method to hunt them. You have a few options based on the geography and vegetation in your area.

Ground blind

Ground blinds are becoming more popular and are an excellent option for areas without many trees. They are easy to set up, keep you hidden from deer, and provide shelter from rain and snow.

Spot and stalk

With this hunting method, you spot deer at a distance before stalking into a range close enough for an effective shot. It's well suited for open spaces like the western parts of the United States and Canada.

Deer stand

A deer stand provides a better view of the surrounding area and makes it more difficult for deer to see or smell you. Stands work well in areas with lots of trees, and they offer some shelter from the weather.

Even if you have the perfect spot, a deer might not come close enough for a shot. You can use these tried-and-true tactics to lure them in when this happens.

What is the rut?

The rut is a three-week mating season that can happen anytime in the fall and winter and peaks in mid-November. Deer are more active and less cautious during this time, making them more responsive to hunting tactics.

Holler back

Bucks communicate by making a grunting sound during the rut. You can mimic this noise by using a deer call and tempting a male deer to investigate.

To pee, or not to pee

The scent of doe urine attracts male deer. You might need to use some urine to get a buck within shooting range.

You wanna fight?

During the rut, bucks fight with each other to establish dominance and attract a mate. You might call in a curious buck by taking a set of antlers and "rattling" them together.

GEAR UP!

You need the right gear to have a comfortable and successful hunt.

Blend in

Camouflage clothing breaks up your outline, making it harder for deer to see you. Also, remember to camouflage your face with a mask or paint.

GEAR CHECKLIST

Required
- Weapon and ammo (gun or bow)
- Deer tag
- Hunting license
- Comfortable boots
- Weather appropriate clothing
- Blaze orange hat and clothing (as required by your state's law)
- Flashlight or headlamp
- Compass or GPS (most cellphones have these)
- Hat

Optional
- Gloves
- Food and water
- Knife
- Rope
- Backpack
- Deer call
- Rattling antlers
- Deer urine
- Cell phone
- Binoculars
- Scent block
- Hand warmers
- Toilet paper (you'll be glad you have it!)

WHAT TO EXPECT ON YOUR FIRST HUNT

The day has come! You've found the perfect location, and you know deer are in the area. You have your gear packed, and you know how to tell the different deer species apart. Now, you get to see if your hard work pays off.

Stay alert

When you first sit down, you'll feel excited, but you will get restless if you go an hour or two without seeing an animal. But stay alert because deer seem to appear when you least expect it.

Buck fever

Here he comes! Your heart pounds, and your hands shake so much that it's hard to hold your gun still. This rush of nerves is called "buck fever," and it happens to most hunters. Take a few deep breaths and try to stay calm.

Field dressing

Once you harvest a deer, you'll need to field dress it as soon as possible to prevent the meat from spoiling. Removing the entrails and internal organs cools down the deer's carcass, keeping it clean and free from bacteria.

HUNTING ETHICS AND RULES

As a hunter, you have the responsibility to obey all laws and ethically harvest wildlife.

Hunting boundaries
Make sure you know the boundaries for your approved hunting area. Do not trespass or shoot at animals on private or restricted land.

Time it right

Know the legal hunting time for the day of your hunt. Even though it may be tempting, do not shoot outside of this time.

Proper identification

"Harvest" means to kill an animal. Only harvest the correct species and sex of deer you have a tag for. Do not shoot a deer you don't have a tag for.

Take aim

Make sure you have a clean shot at the lungs and heart to make an ethical kill. Shooting an animal in the wrong spot can prolong its death and cause unnecessary suffering.

SAFETY FIRST

Along with the fun and thrill of hunting, it is essential to remember that safety comes first. Most areas require a hunter's safety course, which is an excellent way to learn the laws and safe hunting practices.

Where are you?

Tell someone where you will be hunting and when you will be home. Bring along a compass and a cell phone, just in case.

Tree stand safety

Be careful as you enter or exit a tree stand. Always use a harness while you're in the stand. It will keep you safe if you fall or slip.

Can you see me now?
Most areas have laws that require deer hunters to wear blaze orange. The bright orange color makes it easy for other hunters to see you. Thankfully, deer are color blind, so you don't need to worry about the blaze orange giving you away.

GUN SAFETY

All hunters must take gun safety seriously. Guns can be dangerous and can injure someone if you aren't careful. There are over 1,000 hunting-related accidents in the US and Canada every year. Proper safety measures keep you and others from serious injury.

Adult supervision
When practicing gun safety, target shooting, sighting in a rifle, or hunting, always have a responsible adult with you.

The golden rule

Always treat a gun as if it is loaded. Keep it pointed away from people, and don't put your finger on the trigger or turn off the safety catch until you are ready to shoot.

CONSERVATION

Did you know that hunting plays a significant role in wildlife conservation efforts? Hunters love nature and understand the importance of preserving it for future generations.

Hunting fees

Fees paid by hunters fund a variety of conservation programs. These fees have helped deer, turkeys, and many other threatened species recover. They also help preserve wildlife habitats and protect them from poachers, which benefits everyone.

Presidential deer hunter

President Theodore Roosevelt was an avid hunter. He created the first national parks, started conservation programs, and developed the wildlife preserve program.

Population control

Wildlife officials carefully control the number of deer tags sold to hunters, ensuring that deer populations stay within a healthy range.

IT'S GO TIME!

You have the information you need to start your life-long passion as a deer hunter. Remember to stay safe and have fun!

How old are you?

Hunters must be at least 12 years old in most places, but the minimum age may be higher or lower in your area. Check the age requirement in your state or province before going on your first hunt, and always take a responsible adult with you.

Hunter's safety course

Most states and provinces require you to take a hunters safety course before buying a hunting license. The course teaches you about ammunition and firearms, hunting tips, field dressing, hunting laws and regulations, etc.

MOUNT UP!

After a successful hunt, some hunters like to get their deer mounted. Mounts come in various forms and range anywhere from just the antlers to the entire body. It's an excellent way to preserve your memories and show off your prize buck.

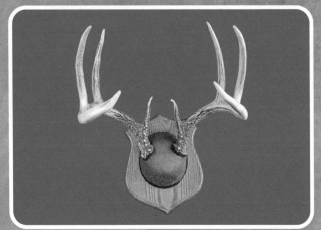

Antler mount
This is the most simple mount, with the antlers displayed on a piece of decorative wood.

European mount
This mount displays the antlers still attached to the exposed skull.

Full-body mount
The entire body of the animal gets mounted for display.

Shoulder mount
This is one of the most popular mounts. It includes the head, neck, and antlers.

RESOURCES

Want to learn more about deer hunting? Here are some books and organizations to check out.

Books to read

Trophy Buck by Art Coulson, illustrated by Johanna Tarkela

Legend of the Ghost Buck (Hometown Hunters) by Lane Walker

The Lost Deer Camp (Hometown Hunters) by Lane Walker

Bowhunting for Kids (Into the Great Outdoors) by Melanie Ann Howard

Join the club

National organizations like the Rocky Mountain Elk Foundation and Backcountry Hunters & Anglers offer educational and friendship opportunities for hunters of all ages. Ask your parents about joining one of them or finding a local club.

GLOSSARY

beam: The main stem of an antler.

blaze orange: A bright orange color hunters use to make themselves more visible to other hunters.

blind: A shelter that keeps hunters hidden from deer.

boundary: A line that marks an area's limit, like a fence, river, or trees.

buck: A male deer.

buck fever: Nervousness that hunters feel when they see deer.

conservation: Protecting the Earth and nature for current and future generations.

doe: A female deer.

downwind: The wind blows toward you and pushes your scent away from the deer.

entrails: An animal's internal organs and intestines.

ethics: The moral values that help people decide what is right and wrong.

field dressing: Removing the internal organs of a harvested animal.

forked antlers: The tines come off the main beam and split into two or more points.

geography: The features, climate, landmarks, and layout of the land.

harvest: To kill an animal.

mount: Preserving an animal for display. See "Taxidermy."

poacher: Someone who hunts or fishes illegally.

private land: Land not owned by federal, state, county, or local governments. A person usually owns private land.

preserve: To keep something in its original state.

public land: Land owned by the government. It can also mean land owned by civilians and managed by the government.

range: The furthest distance that a weapon can accurately hit its target.

rattling: Hitting two antlers together to make a rattling sound, similar to when two male deer fight each other. Curious bucks will come closer to investigate.

restricted land: Land owned by an Indigenous person (Native American) or Indian Tribe. See "Private land."

rub: A spot on a tree where a buck used his antlers to rub off the bark.

rut: The mating season for deer.

safety: A mechanism that prevents a gun from firing accidentally.

scout: To gather information ahead of time.

scrapes: A patch of exposed earth where a buck has pawed the leaves and grass away.

sex: The deer's gender (male or female).

species: Animals with similar genes and appearances.

taxidermy: Preserving an animal by mounting or "stuffing" it for display.

tine: A prong or sharp point on an antler.

trespass: To go onto private or restricted land without permission.

vegetation: The plants that grow in a particular area.

venison: Deer meat.

INDEX

From left to right: Andrew, his dad, and his brother.

About the author

Andrew McMurdie grew up in a hunting family in Wisconsin. Each year, Andrew and his two brothers looked forward to going deer hunting with their father. He loved spending time outdoors and the challenge of deer hunting. Now that he's grown, he enjoys sharing this tradition with his three daughters.

Made in United States
Troutdale, OR
11/17/2024

24939471R00024